DARING WOMEN

— 25 —
WOMEN
WHO
THOUGHT *of* IT FIRST

by Jill Sherman

raintree

a Capstone company — publishers for children

Raintree is an imprint of Capstone Global Library Limited, a company incorporated in England and Wales having its registered office at 264 Banbury Road, Oxford, OX2 7DY – Registered company number: 6695582

www.raintree.co.uk
myorders@raintree.co.uk

Edited by Anna Butzer
Designed by Russell Griesmer
Original illustrations © Capstone Global Library Limited 2019
Picture research by Svetlana Zhurkin
Production by Laura Manthe
Originated by Capstone Global Library Ltd
Printed and bound in India

ISBN 978 1 4747 6253 3
22 21 20 19 18
10 9 8 7 6 5 4 3 2 1

British Library Cataloguing in Publication Data
A full catalogue record for this book is available from the British Library.

Acknowledgements
We would like to thank the following for permission to reproduce photographs: A'Lelia Bundles/Madam Walker Family Archives, 9; Alamy: Guy Corbishley, 33, Kayte Deioma, 29, NASA Image Collection, 47; Courtesy of the Lemelson-MIT Program and Michael Branscom Photography, 7; Getty Images: Condé Nast/Cecil Beaton, 51, The LIFE Images Collection/John Storey, 21, UIG/Universal History Archive, 35; Library of Congress, 11, 27, 53; Mathematical Association of America/Library of Congress, 17; NASA, 19, 20, 39, Paul E. Alers, 41; National Cancer Institute, 57; National Geographic Creative: Hugo van Lawick, cover; Newscom: Reuters/Lucas Jackson, 48, Reuters/Megan Lewis, 45, Sipa/JDD/Bernard Bisson, 31, Zuma Press/Austral/SNAP, 13, Zuma Press/Stanford News Service, 23; Shutterstock: anyaivanova, 5, Elnur, 32, Everett Historical, 37, Ferenc Szelepcsenyi, 46, Kathy Hutchins, 55, Miune, 30, OHishiapply, 15 (right); Smithsonian Institution: National Museum of American History/Graphic Arts Collection, 14; U.S. Fish and Wildlife Service, 43; Wikimedia: U.S. Patent Office, 15 (left)

Design Elements by Shutterstock

CONTENTS

INTRODUCTION

When asked who the greatest scientists in history have been, most people would recall names such as Isaac Newton, Charles Darwin, Thomas Edison and Albert Einstein. Although both men and women are curious about the world around them, women have not always had the same opportunities to explore science. In the past, many women were denied an education. Those who pursued science were not given the opportunity to publish their findings. At other times, men claimed women's findings as their own.

Despite these barriers, some of the greatest scientific minds in history have been women. In the last century, as barriers have fallen, women's contributions to science have exploded. Grace Hopper, for example, is known for creating the first computer language.

Women make up just over 50 per cent of the UK's population, but they make up just 11 per cent of people working in engineering jobs. In addition, they earn less than their male counterparts. As of 2017, men in science and engineering jobs earned an average of £41,200 per year compared to an average of £33,000 for women.

Because of Jane Cooke Wright, we have effective cancer treatments. Stephanie Kwolek's invention of Kevlar has saved the lives of many police officers. Though women's contributions to science have been overlooked in the past, today these intelligent and inquisitive women are celebrated for their many accomplishments.

Technicians in a scientific or medical laboratory must have extensive knowledge of the lab equipment.

Chapter 1

MOTHERS OF INVENTION

Women played a big role in creating many popular products and devices we use today. New inventions are designed to improve the way something is done. Here are just a few of the women whose inventions have improved the lives of millions of people every day.

Stephanie Kwolek
(1923–2014)

When she was young, Stephanie Kwolek's father inspired her with a love of science by taking her on nature walks. Her mother taught her to sew, instilling a love for fabric and sewing. These passions combined in Kwolek's most famous invention, Kevlar.

Kwolek attended Margaret Morrison Carnegie College in Pennsylvania, USA. Graduating in 1946 with a degree in chemistry, Kwolek planned to attend medical school, but she couldn't afford it. Instead, Kwolek searched for a job in chemistry. She was employed in a research position at DuPont USA and

Stephanie Kwolek with a molecular model

began working with polymers. Polymers are large molecules made of smaller units. They are often used to make synthetic materials such as plastics. Kwolek enjoyed the work so much that she decided to stay on at DuPont rather than pursue medical school.

In 1964 DuPont became interested in tyres. Anticipating a fuel shortage, the company thought it would be good to have a new type of lightweight tyre. Kwolek was assigned to work on forming a new synthetic fibre for this purpose.

By mixing two molecules (poly-p-phenylene terephthalate and polybenzamide), Kwolek created a cloudy solution that consisted of liquid crystals. When the solution was heated, it was "spun" into fibres. This new fibre was exceptionally strong. Named Kevlar, it was five times stronger than steel and lighter than fibreglass.

Kevlar was a breakthrough in polymer fibres. Its unique characteristics made it useful for more than just tyres. Kevlar is best known as the material that is used to make bulletproof vests. It is also used for work gloves, skis, fibre optic cables and suspension bridge cables.

Kwolek was awarded 17 patents for her research work. She is one of the most celebrated inventors of her time, receiving numerous awards and honours. In 1994, at the age of 90, Kowlek was inducted into the US National Inventors Hall of Fame.

I guess that's just the life of an inventor: what people do with your ideas takes you totally by surprise.
–Stephanie Kwolek

Madam C.J. Walker

(1867–1919)

Often praised as "the first woman
millionaire in America", Madam C.J. Walker
became famous for her successful line of
haircare products.

Walker did not have the easiest
upbringing. Walker was born Sarah
Breedlove. She was the daughter of
sharecroppers and former slaves in Louisiana,
USA. At the age of seven she became an
orphan. She married at 14 and became a
widow at the age of 20. Then, she and her
two-year-old daughter moved to St. Louis,
Missouri, to live with her brothers. There,
she eventually married her second husband,
Charles J. Walker.

In the 1890s Walker began losing her
hair. She started experimenting with home
treatments to improve the condition. By
1905 she had developed her own tonic and
treatment method that she claimed could
regrow hair. The "Walker system" combined

Madam C.J. Walker, 1914

cleaning the scalp, applying lotions and using iron combs. Her products were made for the specific needs of African-American women's hair. Selling her products directly to other women, she took a personal approach to sales. She gained many loyal customers and an enthusiastic team of saleswomen.

Cosmetic companies had largely overlooked African-American women as customers. By catering to this untapped market, Walker faced little competition for business. Her company became hugely successful. By the time of her death in 1919, Walker's business was worth more than $1 million – that would be more than $14 million today. Her entrepreneurial spirit helped her become the United States' first self-made, female millionaire.

Walker gave back to her community through donations to the National Association for the Advancement of Coloured People (NAACP) and other organizations. Also, by employing African-American women on her sales team, she brought well-paying jobs to her community.

Katharine Burr Blodgett
(1898–1979)

The world became a little bit clearer thanks to Katharine Burr Blodgett's anti-reflective glass coating. Blodgett was a gifted student. She excelled in maths and science. At the age of 15 she won a scholarship to attend the all-female Bryn Mawr College in Pennsylvania, USA. After receiving her master's degree in physics from the University of Chicago in 1918, Blodgett applied for a position at General Electric Laboratories. She was the first female research scientist to be employed by General Electric.

While working at General Electric, Blodgett got the chance to put her passion for science to practical use. After a few years, however, Blodgett took a temporary break from her work at General Electric to continue her studies. In 1924 she travelled to the UK to attend Cambridge University, where she became the first woman at the university to receive a PhD in physics.

In 1926 Blodgett returned to General Electric. She collaborated with chemist Irving Langmuir, who was working on surface chemistry when Blodgett joined him. He had developed a substance that would spread out in a layer of film exactly one-molecule thick when poured onto a surface of water. Working together, Langmuir and Blodgett built on this research, adding the films to metal and glass. This work contributed to Langmuir winning the Nobel Prize in Chemistry in 1932.

Blodgett, however, took this work further, giving it a practical use. She discovered a way to add multiple layers of the film. Blodgett coated materials in up to 44 layers. The glass remained mostly transparent, but was now anti-reflective. These films came to be known as Langmuir-Blodgett films.

This anti-reflective glass was soon used for everything from spectacles to camera lenses. The first cinematic film that

Katharine Burr Blodgett, 1951

was made with Blodgett's anti-reflective glass was *Gone with the Wind*. When it was released in 1939, audiences were amazed by the crisp images on screen. Anti-reflective lenses helped strengthen the film industry with their crystal-clear pictures.

Blodgett's work also helped the US military during World War II (1939–1945). Her anti-reflective glass was used for spy cameras and submarine periscopes. Blodgett's anti-reflective glass is still used today in spectacles, car windscreens and computer monitors.

But that wasn't all Blodgett did. By researching charcoal, she helped improve gas masks, which were also used in World War II. And she developed a method to de-ice the wings of aeroplanes so that pilots could readily fly in subzero temperatures.

Hedy Lamarr
(1914–2000)

During World War II, the US National Inventors Council asked Americans for ideas that would help with the war effort. One surprising responder was the Hollywood actress Hedy Lamarr.

Lamarr knew that radio signals were easily intercepted. She was discussing the problem at a dinner party with the composer George Antheil. Lamarr explained that enemies would find it more difficult to jam signals if they were sent over changing frequencies. Antheil had some experience with frequency hopping from a musical project he had designed. Lamarr and Antheil decided to work together to build a new signalling device. The process was called frequency hopping. It allowed radio transmitters and receivers to change frequencies randomly. This way, anyone listening in would only catch a small part of the conversation. Without knowing what frequency came next, they would be unable to hear the whole thing. In 1942 Lamarr and Antheil were awarded a patent for their device, which could effectively prevent enemies from intercepting messages.

Unfortunately, the US military failed to understand the usefulness of the device in time for it to be used during the war. The navy didn't touch the patent for years. It was finally put into use on navy ships during the Cuban Missile Crisis in 1962. The US military and private companies began developing their own uses for Lamarr's invention. By this point the patent had expired. Neither Lamarr nor Antheil benefited financially from their patent.

Lamarr's work on frequency hopping helped build new technology for wireless communications. Modern technology, such as satellite communication, mobile phones and wireless internet would not be possible without Lamarr's work.

Hedy Lamarr, early 1940s

It wasn't until 1997 that Lamarr was publically recognized for her pioneering work in electronic communications systems. That year, the Electronic Frontier Foundation (EFF) awarded her and Antheil the Pioneer Award, more than 50 years after the device's invention. Lamarr responded, "It's about time."

Knight's model for her automated paper bag machine

Margaret Knight
(1838–1914)

From a young age, Margaret Knight enjoyed working with tools. At home, she often tinkered with kites and sledges. In 1850, when she was 12 years old, Knight visited a cotton mill. Her brothers worked at the mill as overseers, in charge of the workers. While there, Knight saw one of the looms break and the shuttle stabbed the boy who was operating it. This was a common risk associated with the looms.

Knight wanted to fix this problem. She assembled a device to cover the shuttle and to prevent these accidents in the future. Her invention was immediately put into use and sold to other mills across the United States.

Knight's most notable invention came later, in 1868. She was working at the Columbia Paper Bag Company and observed the painstaking process of cutting and folding that was required to make flat-bottomed paper bags. She knew that she could design an easier way. One month later she had sketched an effective design. After another six months, she had assembled a wooden prototype. Operated with a hand crank, the device was much more productive.

Knight took her model to a machine shop, where she worked with machinists to create an iron prototype. A few months later, Knight filed for a patent. But the patent office responded with a rejection. Someone else

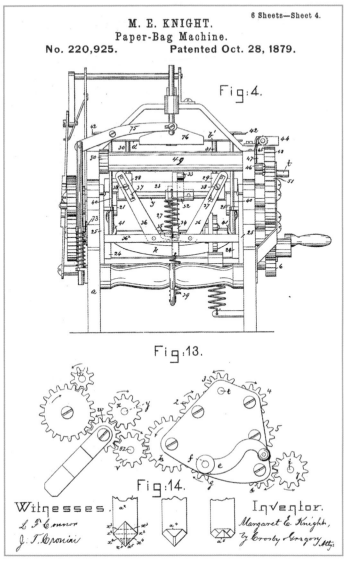

Knight's patent for her paper bag machine

awarded her patent. In 1870 she founded the East Paper Bag company, and set her mind to inventing other things.

Knight's other inventions include six devices used to manufacture shoes, a paper feeding machine, a skirt shield, a clasp for robes and a numbering machine. She was a prolific inventor. In all, she received 27 patents for her various inventions, earning her the nickname "the lady Edison".

Knight's machine folded paper bags similar to this one.

had already filed a patent for the machine. It was Charles Anan, a machinist from one of the shops Knight had worked in to build the prototype. Knight sued Anan. With several witnesses and years' worth of drawings as evidence, Knight won her case and was

Chapter 2

WOMEN YOU CAN COUNT ON

Mathematics is all around us, revealing the logic and the shape of our world. Mathematics is the basis for computers. Though mathematics and computer sciences are subjects dominated by men, women have had an extremely important role in the development of these fields.

Grace Hopper
(1906–1992)

A computer cannot do anything until it is programmed. In order to do that, you need a way to communicate with the computer to tell it what to do. You need a language.

Grace Hopper was a curious and analytical child. When she was seven years old, she wanted to understand how her alarm clock worked. She took it apart, but was unable to put it back together. So she went through her house and took apart seven more alarm clocks. When her mother discovered what she was doing, Grace was limited to taking apart one clock at a time!

At school, Hopper focused on science and mathematics. She attended Vassar College in New York, USA, and later

Grace Hopper, early 1960s

went to Yale University, where she earned her PhD in 1934. Hopper taught at Vassar College until 1943. World War II was raging in Europe and the Pacific, and Hopper felt compelled to join the US Naval Reserve. She joined the division called Women Accepted for Volunteer Emergency Service (WAVES).

Because of her mathematical background, Hopper was assigned to the programming staff at Harvard University working with the new Mark I computer, which performed calculations. This device was 15.5 metres (51 feet) long, 2.4 metres (8 feet) high and weighed more than 4,535 kilograms (10,000 pounds). As with the alarm clocks of her youth, Hopper could hardly wait to discover how it worked. Hopper helped program the Mark I and wrote a 500-page manual for it. After the war, she remained at Harvard, where she worked on the Mark II and Mark III computers.

In the 1950s Hopper started working for the Eckert-Mauchly Computer Corporation. As the senior mathematician overseeing programming on a new computer called UNIVAC I (UNIVersal Automatic Computer I), Hopper was determined to make computer language more accessible. She and her team created a compiler, a program that simplified computer language.

In the early days of computing, programming (working on software) was considered "women's work". Men were employed to develop the hardware. Later, male programmers wanted to elevate their status as programmers. They formed professional organizations for themselves and discouraged companies from employing women. Today, computer programming remains an industry dominated by men.

Next, wanting to create a computer language that understood English, Hopper developed Flow-Matic. Computers operate on a system of of 1s and 0s. Flow-Matic changes the 1s and 0s into "ifs and whens". Flow-Matic led to the development of the widely used Common Business Operating Language (COBOL). Hopper worked on COBOL as well, creating a certifier that translated the language for other computers not running COBOL.

Hopper's work had a profound influence on computer programming. Nicknamed "Amazing Grace", Hopper is an inspiration to many women pursuing careers in science and technology today.

Katherine Johnson
(b. 1918)

In the race to send a man into space, those who worked at NASA had a single focus. This great achievement would not have been possible without the calculations devised by Katherine Johnson.

Katherine Johnson working at her desk at Langley Research Centre in 1966

From a young age, Katherine displayed a passion for numbers. But in 1928, rural West Virginia, USA, offered few educational opportunities for African-American girls. By the age of 10, the local schools would no longer accept her because she was too advanced. So the family moved to Institute, West Virginia, to allow Katherine to attend high school, early. She completed high school at the age of 14, and attended West Virginia State College, where she studied mathematics.

At the age of 35, she was employed as a computer technician with NASA. Before modern computers, people were employed to do the complex calculations needed for space flight. This highly demanding job was the perfect place for Johnson to put her outstanding maths skills to work. Johnson was not content to keep her head down and do the work assigned. For security reasons, NASA blacked out much of the information on the data sheets she was checking. She asked questions. She wanted to know the bigger picture. Her tenacity gained her the respect of her superiors. It was Johnson who calculated the trajectory that put the first US astronaut, Alan Shepard, into space in 1961.

NASA's next major undertaking was to send a man into orbit around Earth. This required much more difficult calculations. She used the geometry of space travel to work out her calculations.

Katherine Johnson was photographed at work at NASA's Langley Research Centre in 1980.

Her work was highly trusted. Even after NASA began using electronic computers, astronaut John Glenn wanted Johnson to confirm the computer's work. He asked that she personally recheck the calculations for his flight orbiting Earth.

Johnson's calculations were also critical to the Apollo moon landing and Space Shuttle programmes. She worked at NASA until 1986. Her work was essential to the success of the space programme. In 2015 she was honoured with the US Presidential Medal of Freedom for her work in space flight. *Hidden Figures,* a film based on Johnson's work and the work of other African-American women at NASA, was released in 2016.

Roberta Williams
(b. 1953)

Women have made some important strides in the tech industry – from software engineering to video game development. Perhaps the most notable female game developer is Roberta Williams.

Roberta Williams, 1993

Roberta Williams was an imaginative child. She often entertained her family with fantasy stories. As an adult, she shared these stories with the aid of technology.

In 1979 Roberta got one of the first home computers, the Apple II. It piqued her interest, and she soon began playing text-based games. It gave her the idea to make a game herself. In 1980 she co-founded a computer gaming company with her husband. Their computer game company, Sierra On-Line, published Williams' first game, *Mystery House,* for the Apple II. It is a simple, graphic adventure game in which the player discovers an abandoned mansion. The player explores the game by typing commands such as "OPEN DOOR" or "LOOK AT TABLE".

The games were sold by mail order, and, to Williams' surprise, *Mystery House* sold more than 10,000 copies. The success allowed Sierra On-Line to expand. Williams soon released two more computer games, *The Wizard and the Princess* and *Time Zones.*

In 1984 IBM hired Williams to develop a new adventure game that people could play again and again. She returned with the first episode in what would become her most famous adventure series. *Kings Quest* was a unique development in gaming. Players could control their characters in two-dimensional space. They could move their characters in front of and behind objects on their screens. In addition, Williams' storytelling had players hooked. She created eight separate adventure games in the Kings Quest series.

Williams is often called the "Queen of the Graphic Adventure". Her work is considered pivotal in game development, and she has been an inspiration for many computer and video game designers.

Maryam Mirzakhani
(1977–2017)

Mathematicians seek elegant solutions to problems. Even solutions to very complex problems can be simplified. One of the women who investigated these solutions was Maryam Mirzakhani.

Mirzakhani grew up in Tehran, Iran. She loved stories and first dreamed of growing up to be a writer. But as she grew older, she began to develop an interest in science and mathematics.

Maryam Mirzakhani, 2012

Mirzakhani became fascinated with mathematics after learning of a solution for adding all the numbers from 1 to 100. This solution was discovered by Carl Friedrich Grauss in the late 1700s. Using this equation, Mirzakhani discovered it was not necessary to add the numbers directly.

Instead, Mirzakhani could use simple multiplication and division to reach the answer more quickly.

As a teenager, Mirzakhani competed in the Mathematical Olympiads. She enjoyed the challenge of solving more complex problems. In 1995 she became the first Iranian student to get a perfect score in the international Mathematics Olympiads competition.

Mirzakhani went on to study mathematics at Sharif University of Technology in Tehran and Harvard University in the United States. After earning her PhD there, she worked at Harvard as a professor and mathematician. Mirzakhani's imagination helped in her work solving complex maths problems. She would form a picture of a complex problem in her head to help her work out the solution.

Mirzakhani's work looks at the heart of geometry in the universe. Though difficult to explain, mathematicians describe her work as breathtaking, superb and ambitious. In 2014 Mirzakhani became the first woman to win the prestigious Fields Medal. The award is often described as the Nobel Prize for mathematics. This extraordinary female mathematician spent her career seeking beauty and elegance in mathematics.

You have to spend some energy and effort to see the beauty in math.
—Maryam Mirzakhani

Carl Friedrich Grauss wasn't a fan of work that had no value. In the late 1700s one of his teachers tried to keep his class busy by adding the numbers 1 to 100. Through straight addition, this task would have taken several minutes. Grauss, instead, devised a formula.

$$\text{Sum from 1 to n} = \frac{n(n+1)}{2}$$

$$\text{Sum from 1 to 100} = \frac{100(100+1)}{2} = (50)(101) = 5050$$

With this formula, Grauss surprised his teacher by delivering a correct answer in just a few seconds. Mirzakhani used this formula in her work.

Chapter 3

WOMEN WHO BUILT IT THEIR WAY

Many extraordinary contributions in the fields of architecture and design have come from women. Women sometimes offer a different perspective on design problems, often considering the social elements of how a building will be used. Here are a few women whose work has transformed the world of architecture and design.

Jane Jacobs
(1916–2006)

Good designs have the power to change the way we interact with the world. Designers plan how to build a product, a building or a city. They must consider how people will use it. A good design will provide users with everything they need. Bad designs will create problems.

Jane Jacobs from the United States did not have any formal training in architecture or urban planning. But she changed the way that we look at our cities. In 1935 Jacobs moved to New York City's Greenwich Village neighbourhood. She came to really appreciate the neighbourhood's town houses, apartments, small businesses and narrow streets. These things, she believed, helped foster a strong sense of community.

By the 1950s landowners and urban planners were eager to develop new building

Jane Jacobs held up documents at a press conference in a fight to save the West Village in New York, USA, on 5 December 1961.

projects. They constructed large apartment buildings and widened the streets. But the communities were suffering. Jacobs was a writer for *Architectural Forum*. In her reporting, she described the effect that modernization had on neighbourhoods. Many people lived in large apartment buildings. City dwellers had to take buses to buy food and get to jobs. These mondernization changes were most frequently carried out in African-American areas. The design was stranding them in lifeless neighbourhoods.

In 1961 Jacobs published *The Death and Life of Great American Cities*. She challenged the urban planning trends of that time. She argued that planning was unnecessary for neighbourhoods to grow. Healthy, vibrant neighbourhoods included pavements, parks, shopfronts, office spaces and apartments.

Jacobs worked hard to preserve neighbourhoods. Throughout the 1960s she fought city planner Robert Moses' proposed highway through lower Manhattan. Moses' expressway would have demolished 416

buildings. In the process, hundreds of families, shops and businesses would be forced out. Jacobs led large public protests to preserve the neighbourhood.

In a time when city planners were bulldozing thriving neighbourhoods, Jacobs argued for their importance. Today she is often considered the architect of the modern city.

Cities have the capability of providing something for everybody, only because, and only when, they are created by everybody.
–Jane Jacobs

Elizabeth Diller

(b. 1954)

From landmarks to museums to experimental art, Elizabeth Diller has been on the cutting edge of architecture. Born in Poland, Diller emigrated to the United States at the age of five. She studied at Cooper Union in New York City, earning her Bachelor of Architecture degree in 1979. Since then she has led the way in exploring how spaces function in our society.

Diller speaking in front of The Broad Museum *on 16 September 2015, prior to the public opening of the museum in Los Angeles, California, USA*

After earning her degree, Diller founded an architecture firm. Diller's early work focused more on artistic pieces that showcase space. For example, in 1981 she arranged 2,500 traffic cones in New York City's Columbus Circle. The piece was designed to draw attention to traffic patterns. In 1986 she designed a stage that contained a mirror. It allowed the audience to see the actors behind a divider.

In 1999 Diller and her firm received a MacArthur Genius Grant. Recipients are awarded money that allows them to pursue unique creative work. Since receiving the grant, the firm has built the Blur Building in Switzerland. This fog-like building was created with jets of water. The massive cloud that resulted fanned out in every direction. Visitors entered a "white-out", not able to clearly see what was in front of them.

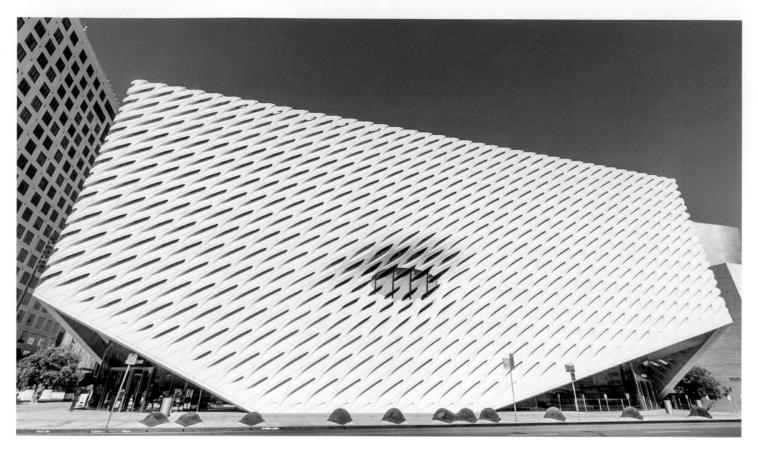

The Broad Museum in Los Angeles, October, 2017

Diller's work isn't always unconventional. Her firm created New York City's High Line. This elevated park was built on the remains of an old freight-train line. It is about 2 kilometres (1.5 miles) long and is very popular with residents and tourists alike. Diller has also completed a redesign of the Lincoln Performing Arts campus in New York City and The Broad Museum in Los Angeles. Diller's unique designs have made her very influential in the world of architecture.

Zaha Hadid
(1950-2016)

Zaha Hadid, a.k.a. "Queen of the Curve", became one of the world's best-known architects. Born in Iraq, Hadid took her inspiration from the beautiful natural landscapes of her home country. Hadid emmigrated to the UK in 1972, and studied at the Architectural Association.

Hadid launched her own firm in 1980. Her drawings were unique and daring, but they were considered too radical to actually be built. In 1988 her drawings were displayed at the Museum of Modern Art in New York City. It wasn't until 1993 that she had a major building constructed. The Vitra Fire Station in Weil am Rhein, Germany, quickly gained international attention. It is composed of soaring planes of exposed concrete. It was unlike anything seen before and quickly became a city landmark.

Not long after this, demand for Hadid's

Zaha Hadid, 2011

skills grew. She became known for her startling, attention-grabbing designs. By the late 2000s, thanks to improved design software, Hadid employed curved forms in her projects. In 2012 she completed her best-known work, The Heydar Aliyev Centre, in Baku, Azerbaijan. The futuristic white wave design is unmistakable.

Hadid was a remarkably innovative

The Heydar Aliyev Centre houses an auditorium, an art gallery and a museum. It is a centre for art and culture in Baku, Azerbaijan. It contains eight floors and the auditorium seats 1,000 people. The design's curves follow the natural contours of the land. They serve as a way to connect the space while also giving each element its own clearly separate identity. The distinct design has made the Heydar Aliyev Centre a landmark of modern Baku.

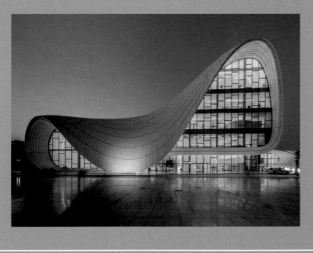

architect. She produced many iconic buildings and her trademark lines and curves make her work easy to identify. Hadid's buildings have left a stunning mark on our modern landscape.

Alison Brooks
(b. 1962)

One of the leading architects today is Alison Brooks. She was born in Canada and studied at the University of Waterloo, graduating in 1988. She later moved to the UK. In 1996 she founded her own architecture firm in London, Alison Brooks Architects.

Brooks is responsible for a number of prize-winning urban design and housing developments. Brooks has designed unique, low-cost housing for those in need. She believes that housing can change lives. In her work, she aims to build homes that make people happy. This was a priority when designing Accordia Living, a housing development in Cambridge.

Alison Brooks standing in front of her design, The Smile, in London, 2016

Brooks understands the need for community. She believes if new homes are to be built in fields, villages should be built around those homes.

One of Brooks's most unique projects is The Smile. This unique, curved "mega tube" was part of the London Design Festival in 2016. It was made using cross-laminated timber (CLT). Lightweight and strong, the project demonstrates CLT's potential as a beautiful and affordable building material.

Brooks is one of the most celebrated architects in the UK. The RIBA Stirling Prize, Manser Medal and Stephen Lawrence Prize are the most prestigious architecture prizes awarded in the UK. Brooks is the only UK architect to have won all three. Her projects continue to showcase thoughtful design and modern architecture.

Chapter 4

WOMEN IN THE LAB

In the field of science, many great discoveries are made through careful investigation. Female scientists work in labs every day. They form hypotheses, conduct experiments and interpret results. Thanks to the many women in science, some of our greatest discoveries have been made.

Rosalind Franklin
(1920–1958)

Rosalind Franklin's work changed our understanding of DNA. Born in London, Franklin knew from the age of 15 that she wanted to be a chemist. She passed the admissions exam for Cambridge University, but her father didn't believe women should go to university. He refused to pay her tuition fees. Eventually, family members convinced him to change his mind. She enrolled at the all-female Newham College in London in 1938.

After graduating from Newham, Franklin planned to continue her studies, but in 1942 World War II was raging and Franklin wanted to contribute. She decided she would be most useful researching carbon and coal for the British Coal Utilisation Research Association.

Rosalind Franklin, 1955

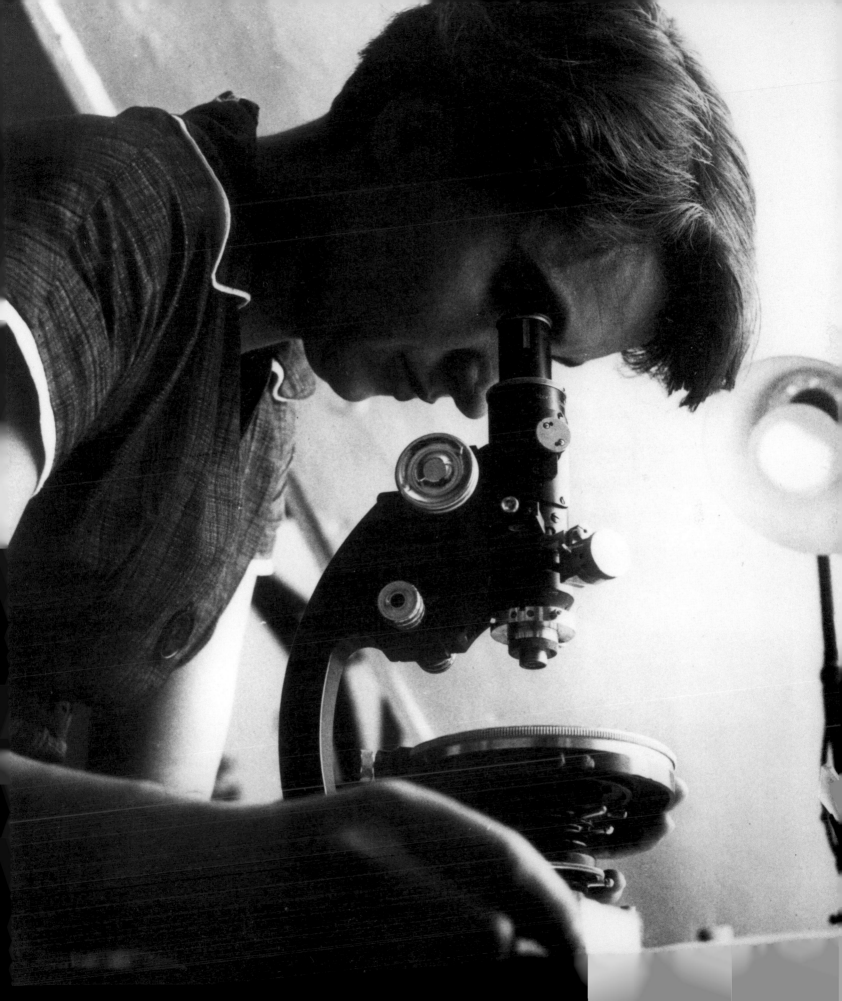

She helped find ways to use coal and charcoal more efficiently.

After the war, Franklin went to Paris, France, where she studied X-ray technology and carbon heating. She returned to London in 1951 to work at Kings College. Franklin used her knowledge of X-rays to study DNA. Soon she uncovered the density of DNA and, more importantly, she discovered that DNA has a helix formation.

One of Franklin's colleagues, Maurice Wilkins, shared Franklin's results with researchers at Cambridge University.

James Watson and Francis Crick were also investigating DNA. Without telling Franklin, Wilkins showed Watson and Crick one of Franklin's photographs. Photo 51 astonished the researchers. They used it as the basis for their DNA model. They published their model in 1953. Franklin's contribution went uncredited.

Franklin died from cancer in 1958. Her cancer was probably caused by her work with X-rays. In 1962 Watson, Crick and Wilkins were awarded the Nobel Prize for their work in discovering the structure of DNA. Though Franklin missed out

DNA (deoxyribonucleic acid) is a molecule found in every cell. It holds the instructions a cell needs to develop, live and reproduce. There are many different types of cells in the human body. DNA tells them what to do. Some give you the sense of taste or touch. Others tell your lungs how to work. DNA also determines such things as what colour eyes you have. Some genes cause disease. Scientists continue to study DNA to better understand the human body.

on the Nobel Prize, many institutions have honoured her work. Today, many academic programmes of study, auditoriums and labs are named after her.

Marie Curie
(1867–1934)

Marie Curie may be the one female scientist everyone has heard of, but not everyone knows what she accomplished. Born in Poland, Marie was the youngest of five children. Her parents were poor schoolteachers, and she had little opportunity for formal education. She worked as a governess and used her earnings to help her sister attend medical school. In 1891 her sister invited her to move to Paris. Once in Paris, Marie attended university at the Sorbonne and studied physics and mathematics.

In 1896 Henri Becquerel discovered radioactivity. He found this energy being released from the element uranium. This new discovery inspired Marie,

Marie Curie, 1898

and she began to research radiation. Marie wanted to know if other elements contained radioactivity. She discovered it in thorium. Soon her husband, Pierre Curie, joined her in her research. Through careful analysis, the Curies discovered two new elements, polonium and radium. In 1903 Becquerel and the Curies were awarded the Nobel Prize for Physics for their discoveries in radiation. Marie became the first woman to receive a Nobel Prize. Marie made history again in 1911 when she became the first person to win a Nobel Prize twice. This time, the award was the Nobel Prize for Chemistry, for her discovery of polonium and radium. She remains the only person to win a Nobel Prize in two different fields.

Curie continued to devote herself to the study of radium. She understood the need to stock radioactive materials. The Radium Institute of the University of Paris was founded in 1914. A supply of radium would be used not just for research, but also for treating cancer.

Over her many years of research, Curie had much direct contact with radium. Scientists such as Curie had yet to learn what precautions were needed when working with radioactive materials. Curie became ill due to her years of radiation exposure. She died in 1934 at the age of 66, but her legacy lives on. Curie is one of the best-known scientists in history.

Peggy Whitson
(b. 1960)

Many discoveries about space can be made in the lab. But some require us to venture into outer space. Peggy Whitson felt the urge to do so. She was first inspired one summer's day in July 1969. She watched Neil Armstrong and Buzz Aldrin make history as they walked on the surface of the Moon.

As of 2017, nearly 900 people had received a Nobel Prize. Only 48 of those people were women.

Whitson took her first steps skywards the next year. Her father took her on her first plane flight. Later, Whitson got into the cockpit, taking flying lessons of her own. She finished high school in 1978. That same year, NASA selected its first female astronauts.

Whitson studied biology and chemistry at Iowa Wesleyan College and Rice University. She applied to be a NASA astronaut in 1986, but was rejected. Undeterred, she kept applying. Whitson began working for NASA as a biochemist in 1989. But her dream was to be an astronaut. She continued to apply for the US astronaut programme every year. Finally, after 10 years of applications, Whitson was accepted in 1996. After two years of training, she began working in the planning branch.

Whitson continued dreaming of going into space. In 2002, after years of hard work

Whitson floated through the Unity *module aboard the International Space Station on 28 November 2016.*

and training, Whitson was chosen for a space mission. She rocketed into space, docking at the International Space Station (ISS). She and the crew installed new machinery. Whitson performed experiments investigating life science and microgravity. After six months in space, Whitson returned to Earth. But that was not her last trip to space.

Whitson returned to the ISS in 2007 when another group of astronauts was leaving. They handed over command of ISS to Whitson. She is the only woman to have held this position. She held this position again during her third space mission, which began in November 2016. She returned to Earth for the final time, in September 2017, at the age of 57. Nicknamed the Space Ninja, she has logged an incredible 665 days in space. That's more time in space than any other US astronaut.

> *The most important thing about the station is the friendships and the work we accomplish there.*
> —Peggy Whitson

Sara Seager
(b. 1971)

Sara Seager's eyes have always been firmly fixed on the stars. One of her earliest memories is of a "star party" with her father. She got to look at the Moon through a telescope. It was stunning!

Seager bought her own telescope when she was 16. She focused her studies on science, attending the University of Toronto in Canada. She went on to earn a PhD in Astronomy from Harvard University in 1999. It was during this period that the first reports came out about exoplanets. Scientists had spotted what appeared to be planets revolving around faraway stars. Seager decided to study the atmospheres around these planets. Not all scientists were convinced, however. They thought the sightings could be the result of star

The first woman in space was Soviet cosmonaut Valentina Tereshkova in 1963. Sally Ride, the first American woman to reach space, did so in 1983. The first European woman, Helen Sharman from the UK, followed in 1991.

variability. But exoplanets kept being spotted. With this growing scientific evidence, Seager's work was validated.

Since then, Seager has been able to refine the detection of exoplanets. Her predictions led to the Hubble Telescope's first detection of an exoplanet atmosphere. So far, Seager has discovered more than 700 exoplanets. But she has a bigger goal in mind. Seager wants to find a planet similar to Earth. By looking at exoplanet atmospheres, she can gauge the planet's temperature and composition. Seager is eager to find Earth-like planets. Exploring those planets more closely could reveal signs of extraterrestrial life.

Seager is spearheading project ASTERIA. The project has deployed small space telescopes past Earth's atmosphere. With a clear picture of the sky from outer space, the telescopes will be better positioned to hunt exoplanets than they would be on Earth. Seager believes that there is definitely life on other planets and the discovery of extraterrestrial life may happen sooner than we might believe.

Seager at a press conference at NASA headquarters in Washington, D.C., on 6 April 2009

Chapter 5

EARTH ENTHUSIASTS

Down here on Earth, scientists explore the environment. Looking to nature, scientists can discover information about Earth's past and make predictions about its future.

Rachel Carson
(1907–1964)

Rachel Carson grew up on a farm in Pennsylvania, USA. Living in a rural environment, Carson was always close to nature and wildlife. She attended the Pennsylvania College for Women, planning to become a writer. But her love of nature drew her into the field of biology. She graduated in 1929 and then began working on her masters at Johns Hopkins University in Baltimore, Maryland, USA. Carson earned her degree in zoology in 1932.

She intended to continue her studies to earn a PhD, but in 1935 Carson's father died. Her family needed financial help, so Carson taught for several years. In 1936 Carson joined the US Fish and Wildlife Service. There, she was able to combine her love of nature with writing. Carson wrote scripts for the department's

Rachel Carson, 1940s

radio programme. People loved them. Carson made the scientific subject matter interesting and understandable.

Soon Carson began submitting articles about wildlife to magazines. In 1941 she published her first book. *Under the Sea-Wind* described the interactions between a bird, a fish and an eel. Critics were impressed. Her prose was clear and elegant, and the material was not overly technical.

In 1951 she published her second book, *The Sea Around Us*. It was a great success. Excerpts were printed in magazines, and sales took off. She even won the 1952 US National Book Award for Non-fiction. Her third book, *The Edge of the Sea*, was published in 1955.

Now a full-time writer, Carson turned her attention away from the sea. She wanted to tackle the issue of pesticides. Carson tracked the impact pesticides had on the environment. Her book *Silent Spring* was published in 1962. It opened many

people's eyes to the negative effects of chemicals on nature. Chemical companies called her an alarmist. But a special task force investigated and endorsed her findings.

Carson died in 1964. She would not see the impact her work had on the world. Carson's words emphasized the need to protect our environment. Many believe that without her influence organizations such as the United States' Environmental Protection Agency would not exist today.

> Those who dwell among the beauties and mysteries of the earth are never alone or weary of life.
> —Rachel Carson

Jane Goodall
(b. 1934)

Studying animals in the wild takes patience. This is a lesson Jane Goodall learned as a young girl. When she was four years old, her parents reported her missing. They found her hours later, crouched in a henhouse. Jane had been sitting there for hours watching the hens. She wanted to see how they laid their eggs.

Jane Goodall observing chimpanzees at Taronga Zoo in 1997, in Sydney, Australia. Taronga Zoo has since established a partnership with the Jane Goodall Institute to promote the rehabilitation of orphaned chimpanzees back into the wild.

Goodall has been fascinated by animals her whole life. As a child, Goodall read the fictional Doctor Doolittle books by Hugh Lofting and felt inspired to travel to Africa. She wanted to see animals in their natural habitats. She got her wish in 1957. A friend invited Goodall to visit her in Africa.

There, Goodall met the famous scientist Louis Leakey. Leakey was interested in the origins of humans. He thought it would be a good idea to study the primates most closely related to humans. He believed Goodall had the right mind for this work. He employed her to observe chimpanzees in the wild.

In 1960 Goodall set up a camp on the Gombe Stream Reserve in Tanzania. She found a group of chimps. They were frightened by her presence and she couldn't get close enough to watch them. So Goodall found another group. This time, she was more cautious. She kept her distance and arrived at the same time every day. The chimps began to tolerate her presence. Gradually, Goodall moved closer. After a year, the chimps

Jane Goodall after speaking at Millenaris Teatrum on 17 May 2009, in Budapest, Hungary

allowed her to get as close as 9 metres (30 feet) away. After two years they didn't mind her at all. In fact, because she began taking bananas, they often came right up to her looking for a treat.

No other scientist had got this close to chimpanzees in the wild before. Goodall changed the way scientists thought of chimps. For example, scientists had believed that chimps were vegetarian. But Goodall witnessed them eating meat from a pig. She also saw them hunt and kill a monkey. Goodall discovered that chimps make and use tools, defend their territory and even use a primitive type of language.

National Geographic magazine published Goodall's work. Goodall became a celebrity. She appeared in magazines and on television programmes. She began to devote her attention to educating the public. She wants people to understand that chimpanzees' habitats are in danger. Goodall continues to fight for better treatment of chimpanzees in captivity. She believes animals should be treated better by scientists.

Adriana Ocampo
(b. 1955)

Even as a child, Adriana Ocampo loved the stars. Brought up in Argentina, Ocampo would go out onto the roof of her house at night. Looking up at the stars she would wonder how far away they were. When Ocampo played with her dolls, she would turn them into astronauts. Kitchen utensils became spaceships.

She emigrated to the United States in 1970. A few years later, when she was 18 years old, Ocampo got a summer job working at NASA's Jet Propulsion Laboratory (JPL). She studied pictures of Mars sent back from the *Viking* spacecraft.

In 1980 Ocampo became a US citizen. In 1983 she earned a geology degree from California State University. All the while, she continued to work at JPL. After university, she began working there full time as a research scientist.

NASA missions are huge efforts. Many people work together to get everything just right. Ocampo was involved in the planning of several missions. She was involved in the Mars Observer project, Voyager mission and Project Galileo. Her background in geology helped her to analyse pictures of distant moons.

Her biggest discovery, however, was much closer to home. Scientists have long believed that a massive asteroid hit Earth millions of years ago. The massive cloud of dust would have blocked out the Sun. Dinosaurs and other life would have been decimated. But there was one problem with

Adriana Ocampo, 2014

this idea – if this asteroid had hit Earth, where was the crater?

In 1989 Ocampo was studying Mexico's Yucatán Peninsula. She did so the same way she studied distant moons. She used satellite pictures. Ocampo was using the images to map water resources. But she noticed something unusual. She spotted a semicircular ring of sinkholes.

Several scientists before had found unusual formations and minerals in that area, called Chicxulub. They guessed that it could be the site of a huge crater.

Ocampo's evidence helped to prove it. The crater was 193 km (120 miles) wide.

Ocampo continued to study the Chicxulub crater. She even visited Mexico to explore nearby sites on the ground. Her research has led to exciting new discoveries. Scientists have determined that the asteroid that hit Chicxulub was around 9 to 13 kilometres (6 to 8 miles) wide. It would have caused a global cloud of sulphuric acid. And that dark cloud would have hung in Earth's atmosphere for about 10 years.

The Chicxulub crater is one of the most exciting discoveries of Earth's geology. Ocampo continues to study the crater. She hopes to learn more about how Earth and the solar system formed. The crater may even hold clues to how life evolved on Earth.

Katharine Hayhoe
(b. 1972)

Some of the most important scientific questions today are about climate change. Katharine Hayhoe is investigating those

Katharine Hayhoe attended the TIME *100 gala in New York, USA, on 29 April 2014.*

questions. When most people think about climate change, they think about melting ice, the north and south poles and the animals that live there. But Hayhoe wants to be able to explain what climate change means for us in the places we live.

Hayhoe studied atmospheric science at the University of Illinois, USA, earning a PhD. She has written more than 125 peer-reviewed academic works. In addition to research, Hayhoe is especially interested in talking to climate-change sceptics.

Hayhoe is an evangelical Christian and a scientist. So she understands how difficult it can be to reach people when science seems to conflict with religion. Because some people think climate change is a hoax, there is a lot of bad information being spread around. Even though most scientists agree about climate change, people continue to doubt its effects.

Hayhoe explains that climate change is already happening. In her home state of Texas, she cites evidence such as sea level rise and stronger storms. How much these things will change in the future depends on what we do now. Carbon emissions, for example, have a big effect. If we can reduce our carbon output, we may be able to keep the climate in check.

In 2009 Hayhoe published her first book, *A Climate for Change*. In it, she answered common questions that many people have about climate change. And she provided evidence to show its cause and how we can change it.

Her work is having a big impact. In 2014 Hayhoe was named one of *TIME* magazine's 100 Most Influential People. As long as climate change continues to be questioned by non-scientists, Hayhoe will continue to work on sharing evidence beyond the scientific community.

During a peer review, experts analyse the data presented by the scientist or scientists who have performed the study. When an article is submitted to a journal, it must be validated. Experts ensure that the work is properly researched. They check that the conclusions make sense. A badly designed experiment will give bad results. And if scientists ignore some results in favour of others, they will present the wrong conclusions. Peer-reviewed journals make sure accurate science is being published.

Chapter 6

OUR BODIES, OUR MINDS

Women haven't always been allowed access to medical training. Yet, they often have the informal role of carer. Since the 1800s, women have made great strides in the study of illness and mental health. New insights and treatments developed by women have helped, and continue to help, thousands of people.

Mamie Phipps Clark
(1917–1983)

Growing up in Alabama, USA, during the early 1900s, Mamie Phipps Clark was no stranger to racism. Her father was a doctor and her family was financially comfortable, but she attended segregated schools. When she finished high school at the age of 16 in 1934, many African Americans still had few opportunities for higher education.

In 1934 Clark enrolled in the all-black Howard University in Washington, D.C. She began studying maths and physics, but soon took an interest in psychology. She went on to earn her PhD in psychology from Columbia University in New York. Clark was the first African-American woman to earn a PhD in psychology from Columbia University.

Mamie Phipps Clark, 1968

As part of her work, Clark started a project to look at young African-American children. She wanted to learn how these young boys and girls understood their race. She designed a study to see what colour dolls African-American children preferred. She researched children from segregated schools in the south of the United States as well as children from integrated schools in the north-east.

In the experiment, children from the ages of three to seven were offered four dolls. Two of the dolls had brown skin and black hair. The other two had white skin and yellow hair. The children were asked: "Which doll do you want to play with? Which doll looks nice? Which doll looks bad? Which doll looks like you?"

Most of the children said the white dolls were nice. They thought the black dolls were bad – even though the black dolls looked like them. Clark published her results in 1950. She found that the children became aware of their race at the age of three. At the same time, they began to see themselves negatively in society.

Clark's work was presented at trials to desegregate schools. It was even cited at the US Supreme Court hearing for *Brown v. Board of Education of Topeka* in 1954. In this landmark case, the Court ruled that segregation in the schools was unlawful.

Clark saw the deep emotional impact of racism. She opened The Northside Centre for Child Development in New York City. She also helped launch the Head Start programme. These initiatives offer social services education programmes to low-income families. Clark's work has greatly improved the lives of countless African-American children.

Jane Cooke Wright

(1919–2013)

Parents are often a source of inspiration. Both Jane Cooke Wright and her sister Barbara followed in their father's footsteps by joining the medical profession. Louis Wright was one of the first African Americans to graduate from Harvard Medical School. He was also the first African American doctor appointed to the staff of a New York City hospital.

Wright graduated from New York Medical College in 1945. She trained at Harlem Hospital. Eventually, she joined her father working on cancer research.

Cancer has many forms. It involves abnormal cell growth. It usually starts in one part of the body as a tumour, or mass

Jane Cooke Wright, 1958

of abnormal cells. But cancer can spread across the body. Wright began researching cancer treatments in 1949. The Wrights started looking into an experimental treatment called chemotherapy. At the time, chemotherapy was a last resort treatment. Many different types of drugs were being used in chemotherapy. And the drugs were still being developed. Dosages were also poorly understood.

The Wrights tested various drugs. Chemotherapy treatments take a toll on the patient. The drugs are toxic. Depending on the drugs they used, the Wrights adjusted doses and changed the length of treatment.

The results were remarkable. Many types of cancer were improved. Blood cancers, for example, were thought to be incurable. But the Wrights saw patients go into partial remission. The treatment had an effect and patients had less cancer in their bodies. It was groundbreaking research.

In 1952, after her father's death, Wright became the head of the US Cancer Research Foundation. She looked for ways to select the right drugs. She started to biopsy tumours. In a biopsy, a doctor will remove some of the diseased cells or tissue. Then they examine the cells under a microscope. Wright tested different drugs on the cells in a lab. By understanding a particular tumour, Wright could select the best drug for treatment.

In addition, Wright fought for access to medical care in the United States. Beginning in 1964, she worked with a presidential commission on communicating new research to hospitals nationwide. Wright's work has had a lasting impact. It has formed the basis for all modern chemotherapy research. Countless people have benefited from her work and are alive today because of it.

Temple Grandin
(b. 1947)

Temple Grandin was not a typical child. At the age of two, the age when most children begin talking, she was unusually quiet. She also disliked being touched and was prone to tantrums. Concerned, her mother took her to the doctor. Grandin was diagnosed with brain damage. Doctors recommended she be placed in an institution. But her parents paid for private education. Her mother soon realized that many of Grandin's symptoms were consistent with autism. Grandin began speech therapy. It took two years before Grandin began talking at the age of four.

Temple Grandin arrives at the HBO Golden Globe Party on 16 January 2011, in California, USA. Some people know her from the HBO biopic, Temple Grandin.

When she was 18, Grandin visited her aunt's cattle ranch. She noticed the cows entering a squeeze chute. It held the cows while they were vaccinated and branded. Fascinated, Grandin built herself a similar machine. Using her "hug machine", she could control the amount of pressure. The machine's hugs helped her deal with stress.

Despite her behavioural issues, Grandin did very well at school. She studied psychology at Franklin Pierce College. Then she went on to earn a PhD in animal science from Arizona State University in 1989.

Just as most autistic people are hypersensitive to sound and touch, so are animals. Grandin wanted to use her insight to help both humans and animals. A version of Grandin's "hug machine" is now commonly used to soothe people with autism. Grandin also works with livestock companies to improve quality of life for cows.

As Grandin has difficulty in social situations, she prefers to work alone. She started her own company, Grandin Livestock Handling Systems. She has designed systems for companies such as McDonald's. The cows are treated better and are not as stressed compared with less humane systems. Though animals remain a part of many people's diets, compassionate systems make animal treatment more humane.

I think using animals for food is an ethical thing to do, but we've got to do it right.
–Temple Grandin

Flossie Wong-Staal

(b. 1947)

AIDS is one of the world's most devastating diseases. There is no known cure. Worldwide, more than 35 million people have died of AIDS since it was discovered in 1983. It is no surprise that scientists are focused on learning more about the disease.

Flossie Wong-Staal was born in China, but in 1952 her family fled to Hong Kong to escape communism. In Hong Kong, Wong-Staal attended an all-girls Catholic school where she was able to study science. Wong-Staal made her family proud by doing well in exams. None of the women in her family had attended university, but her family supported the idea. In 1965 Wong-Staal emigrated to

Flossie Wong-Staal, 2010

the United States to study at the University of California in Los Angeles. She earned her PhD in molecular biology in 1972.

After completing her education, Wong-Staal took a job working at the National Cancer Institute. She began working with AIDS researcher Robert Gallo. Together they studied retroviruses. These viruses insert their DNA into healthy cells. When those cells replicate, the virus spreads.

In 1983 Wong-Staal and others identified HIV, the virus that causes AIDS. They were then able to create a map of the virus's genes. This was a groundbreaking step in the fight against AIDS. Finally, researchers could test patients for the virus.

So far, HIV and AIDS have been difficult to combat. The virus changes rapidly and becomes resistant to drug treatments. Wong-Staal continues to look for ways to fight the disease. Her focus is on understanding the genes that allow the virus to infect human cells.

It adds to the joy of discovery to know that your work may make a difference in people's lives.
—Flossie Wong-Staal

Timeline

1870 Margaret Knight founds the East Paper Bag company, using an invention of her design

1903 Marie Curie becomes the first woman awarded the Nobel Prize for her discoveries in radiation

1905 Madam C.J. Walker develops her hair tonic and treatment method, launching a business that makes her the first female millionaire in the United States

1938 Katharine Burr Blodgett develops a technique to make anti-reflective glass

1942 Hedy Lamarr and George Antheil receive a patent for their frequency hopping communications device, which is the precursor to satellite communications and Wi-Fi

1949 Jane Cooke Wright begins researching drugs for chemotherapy treatment

1952 Rosalind Franklin's Photograph 51 helps reveal the structure of DNA

1954 Mamie Phipps Clark's doll study is cited in *Brown v. Board of Education of Topeka*

1959 Grace Hopper and her team develop the COBOL computer language

1960 Jane Goodall sets up a camp on the Gombe Stream Reserve in Tanzania and begins her study of chimpanzees

1961 Katherine Johnson calculates the trajectory that puts the first US astronaut, Alan Shepard, into space

1961 Jane Jacobs publishes *The Death and Life of Great American Cities*

1962 Rachel Carson's *Silent Spring* is published

1965 Stephanie Kwolek discovers a technique to make very strong, lightweight fabric, now called Kevlar

1984 Roberta Williams develops *Kings Quest*, a new, replayable adventure game

1989 Adriana Ocampo identifies sinkholes indicating the Chicxulub crater

1991 Helen Sharman becomes the first European woman in space

2002 Elizabeth Diller installs the formless, fog-like Blur Building in Switzerland

2007 Sara Seager wins the Helen B. Warner Prize for developing fundamental techniques for understanding the atmospheres of exoplanets

2008 Alison Brooks wins the RIBA Stirling Prize for her design of Accordia Living

2012 Zaha Hadid completes the curved Heydar Aliyev Centre in Baku, Azerbaijan

2014 Maryam Mirzakhani becomes the first female mathematician to win the Fields Medal for her work in complex geometry

Glossary

autism condition that causes people to have trouble communicating and forming relationships with others

biopsy removal of body tissue for scientific study

chemotherapy treatment of disease, especially cancer, with chemicals

DNA material in cells that gives people their individual characteristics; DNA stands for deoxyribonucleic acid

element something that cannot be broken down into simpler substances

entrepreneur person who begins his or her own business

exoplanet planet that orbits a star outside of the solar system

gene part of a cell that controls a living thing's characteristics and growth

molecule smallest particle into which a substance can be divided without being changed chemically

patent legal document giving someone sole rights to make or sell a product

polymer artificial material such as plastic or resin that is created using chemicals

primate any animal in the group of mammals that includes humans, apes and monkeys

programming writing a list of instructions for a computer to follow

prototype first version of a new invention from which other versions are developed

radiation tiny particles sent out from radioactive material

remission state in which a disease is no longer detectable

sharecropper farmer who works the land in exchange for housing and part of the profits

synthetic not natural, made by combining different substances

trajectory curved path of an object in space

urban planning process of determining how land should be used in urban environments

Comprehension questions

1. Hedy Lamarr's frequency hopping patent was ignored for decades. How does this compare to Rosalind Franklin's lack of recognition for her work in DNA?
2. Why should inventors document their work? How did this help Margaret Knight get a patent on her paper bag folding machine?
3. Why do you think that most famous scientists have been men?

Find out more

Books

100 Scientists Who Made History (DK Science), Andrea Mills (DK Children, 2018)

Jane Goodall: Chimpanzee Protector (Women in Conservation), Robin S. Doak (Raintree, 2015)

Marie Curie (Against the Odds), Claire Throp (Raintree, 2016)

Rachel Carson: Environmental Pioneer (Women in Conservation), Lori Hile (Raintree, 2015)

Websites

Find out more about Rosalind Franklin at:
www.dkfindout.com/uk/science/famous-scientists/rosalind-franklin

Learn more about women astronauts from the European Space Agency at:
www.esa.int/About_Us/Welcome_to_ESA/ESA_history/50_years_of_humans_in_space

Source notes

Pages 6–7: Kelsey D. Atherton. "Stephanie Kwolek, Kevlar Inventor, Dead at 90." Popular Science. June 20, 2014, https://www.popsci.com/article/science/stephanie-kwolek-kevlar-inventor-dead-90

Pages 9–10:
"Madam C.J. Walker." History. 2009, https://www.history.com/topics/black-history/madame-c-j-walker

Henry Louis Gates, Jr. "Madam Walker, the First Black American Woman to Be a Self-Made Millionaire." PBS. 2014, http://www.pbs.org/wnet/african-americans-many-rivers-to-cross/history/100-amazing-facts/madam-walker-the-first-black-american-woman-to-be-a-self-made-millionaire

Pages 12–13: Rebecca Greenfield. "Celebrity Invention: Hedy Lamarr's Secret Communications System." The Atlantic. September 3, 2010, https://www.theatlantic.com/technology/archive/2010/09/celebrity-invention-hedy-lamarrs-secret-communications-system/62377/

Pages 16–19: "Grace Hopper Biography." Biography. February 27, 2018, https://www.biography.com/people/grace-hopper-21406809

Pages 19–21: "Katherine Johnson: The Girl Who Loved to Count." NASA. November 24, 2015, https://www.nasa.gov/feature/katherine-johnson-the-girl-who-loved-to-count

Pages 23–24: "Meet the First Woman to Win Math's Most Prestigious Prize." Quanta Magazine. August 13, 2014, https://www.wired.com/2014/08/maryam-mirzakhani-fields-medal/

Pages 26–28: Marc Weingarten. "Jane Jacobs, the Writer Who Changed the Face of the Modern City." The Guardian. 2016, https://www.theguardian.com/books/2016/sep/21/jane-jacobs-modern-city-biography-new-york-greenwich-village

Pages 31–32: Pat Finn. "From A to Zaha: 26 Women Who Changed Architecture." Architizer. 2017, https://architizer.com/blog/inspiration/industry/from-a-to-zaha-26-women-who-changed-architecture/

Pages 38–40: Amy B. Wang. "Astronaut Peggy Whitson Has Returned to Earth, a Couple More NASA Records in Hand." The Washington Post. September 5, 2017, https://www.washingtonpost.com/news/speaking-of-science/wp/2017/09/05/astronaut-peggy-whitson-has-returned-to-earth-a-couple-more-nasa-records-in-hand/?utm_term=.25dd0dc87ce7

Pages 45–46: "Jane Goodall." Britannica. July 20, 1998. https://www.britannica.com/biography/Jane-Goodall

Select bibliography

Ayers, Andrew. Safe as Houses. Architectural Review. Vol. 240 Issue 1433, p136-144, 2016.

Goodall, Jane. *The Chimpanzees I Love: Saving Their World and Ours.* New York: Scholastic Press, 2001.

McGrayne, Sharon Bertsch. *Nobel Prize Women in Science: Their Lives, Struggles, and Momentous Discoveries.* Washington DC: Joseph Henry Press. 2001.

Roberts, Jason. Peggy A. Whitson (PH.D.) NASA Astronaut. *NASA.* 27 Sept 2017. https://www.nasa.gov/astronauts/biographies/peggy-a-whitson/biography

Swaby, Rebecca. *Headstrong: 52 Women Who Changed Science—and the World.* New York: Broadway Books. 2015.

About the author

Jill Sherman lives and writes in Brooklyn, New York, USA. She has written several books for young people. She enjoys researching new topics and is thrilled to be sharing the accomplishments of outstanding female scientists with young readers. Jill is training to run a 10K and enjoys taking photos of her dog.

Index